THE REAL GOD

Carefully avoid the things that can become false gods. Begin at Enter and find your way through the castle's maze to the One True God.

ONE TRUE GOD

PLEASURE

LEARNING

SPORTS

POWER

FOOD

MONEY

FUN

TV

CLOTHES

FRIENDS

ENTER

KEY VERSE

Psalm 95:3

REal LOVE

Use the code found in the hearts to decode this message that tells us how much God loves us.

```
 1  3  2            8  3  7  6  2
 6  7  6  5  4  3  12  6      11  12      9  10  6
13  3  5  8  2      16  3      14  15  17  10      9  10  18  9
10  6      1  18  7  6      10  11  16      3  12  8  4
16  3  12      9  3      2  11  6 ;      12  3  13
18  12  4  3  12  6      13  10  3
19  6  8  11  6  7  6  16      11  12
10  11  14      13  11  8  8      12  3  9
 2  11  6      19  15  9
13  11  8  8      8  11  7  6
20  3  5  6  7  6  5
```

G/1 D/2 O/3 Y/4 R/5 E/6 V/7 L/8 T/9 H/10 I/11 N/12 W/13 M/14 U/15 S/16 C/17 A/18 B/19 F/20

KEY VERSE

John 3:16

REAL HELP

HEALING

Look at the pictures showing that Jesus healed many people of all kinds of sicknesses. Find and circle 10 things in picture 2 that are different from picture 1.

Picture 1

Picture 2

KEY VERSE

Luke 4:40

Real Life

Read the account of Jairus' daughter in Luke 8:51–55. Then number the pictures in the correct order to show what happened.

People outside crying.

Girl is healed.

Jesus arrives at Jairus' house.

People laugh at Jesus.

Jesus touches girl's hand.

Peter, John, James, and parents enter house.

KEY VERSE

Luke 8:51–55

Real Today

Read this paraphrase of what the Bible says can happen today. Then fit the bold words into the correct boxes of the puzzle with the letters already provided. Read the words in the shaded boxes to see what God wants us to believe for from Him.

Is anyone **sick**? He should call **people** in the **church** and they will **anoint** him with **oil** and **pray** over him in the name of the Lord.

The **prayer** of those who **believe** will **heal** the sick and the Lord will raise him up. If he has committed any **sins**, he will be **forgiven**.

Confess your sins to each other, and pray for each other that you can be **healed**. The **sincere**, **urgent** prayer of a **righteous** person will achieve **results**.

5

KEY VERSE

James 5:14–16

A Big Family

Jesus wants everyone to become part of God's family. Find and circle the words in the list that are hidden in the letters that are in the cross. Print the leftover letters from left to right on the spaces below to see what the Bible says about becoming part of His family.

BELIEVE   **SALVATION**
JESUS   **CROSS**
HEAVEN   **THORN**
SINS   **DIED**
BLOOD   **SACRIFICE**

REPENT   **NAILS**
LIFE   **WORLD**
SAVED   **REDEEMED**
GRACE   **FAITH**
EVERLASTING

```
          A N Y O N E
          W H O E B E
          E S A V E D
          C L I E E V
E S A L V A T I O N R S W O R L D I N A N
D I A I C C E F H A L P T S J E I S U S W
I N L F L B E I E I A E V E I L E B C O M
E S A E P A R R A L S T H O R N D O O L B
          C V S T N D
          A E S I E E
          S N O N P M
          T O R G E E
          F G C R R E
          H T I A F D
          O D S C F E
          A M I E L R
          Y J E S U S
```

Jesus loves the world so much!

_ _ _ _ _ _ _ _

_ _ _ _ _ _ _ _

_ _ _ _ _ _ _

_ _ _ _ _ _ _

_ _ _ _ _ _ _

_ _ _ _ _ _ _ '

_ _ _ _ _ _ .

KEY VERSE

John 1:12

A Big Problem

SALVATION

Hold this page flat at your eye level and look at the puzzle from the numbered arrows to find the words to complete the following sentences.

1. Everyone has _____.

2. The _____ of sin is death.

3. Everyone needs to be _____.

4. Jesus _____ everyone.

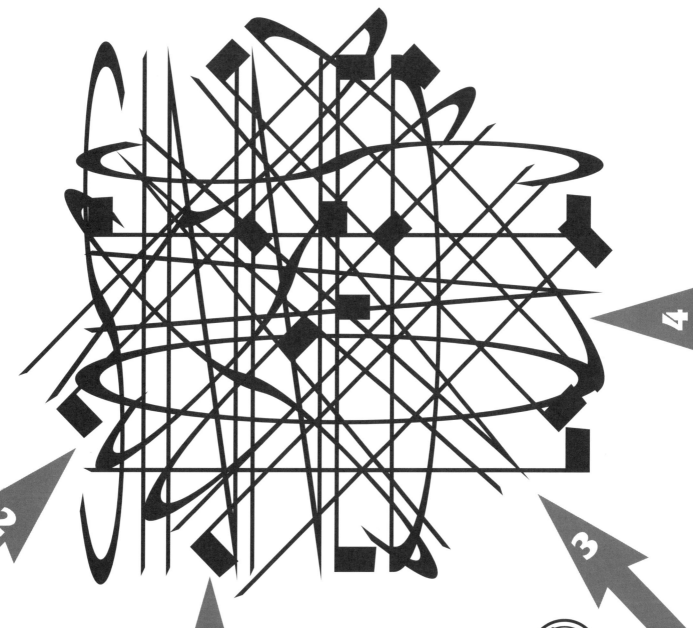

KEY VERSE

Romans 3:23; 6:23

SALVATION

Hurting someone keeps you from having the same friendship with that person that you had before. Every person sins, and sin hurts God. It breaks our relationship with Him. Follow the directions below to see how we can get rid of the sin that keeps us from having a right relationship with Him. The boxes are in numbered rows and columns that have letters. For example, 1A is the box with the word *fight* in it.

If Jesus is God, color boxes 1a, 5E, 8B, 6D, 7A green.

If God loves everyone, color boxes 8A, 1B, 7E, 5A, 2E red.

If God created the world, color boxes 1D, 6A, 9E, 4D yellow.

If God has all power, color boxes 9A, 5D, 2B, 4A, 6E, 8D blue.

If God is holy, color boxes 1E, 4B, 6B, 8E, 9D, 2A purple.

If sin hurts God, color boxes 9B, 2D, 4E, 7B, 5B, 7D orange.

	A	B	C	D	E
1	FIGHT	ANGER	ONLY	SAD	ONLY
2	JESUS	GOD	JESUS'	HATE	LOVE
3	BLOOD	CAN	REMOVE	OUR	SINS
4	BIBLE	EARTH	AND	BLOOD	SPIRIT
5	HURT	SINS	RESTORE	FRIENDS	GOD
6	LOVE	HEAVEN	OUR	HOLY	REMOVE
7	SPIRIT	OUR	FRIENDSHIP	PAIN	RESTORE
8	FORGIVE	GOD	WITH	ANGER	ETERNAL
9	SINS	BLOOD	GOD	CAN	FORGIVE

Romans 5:8

8

THE WAY

SALVATION

Follow the correct letter path to see who can be saved. Write the letters on the spaces below.

B R E V E O H W E V E G I F T S S
E   R   R   O
V   E   Y   F
E   V   O   G
C S L L I W H O E S W H O C A
E   H   B   L
M   A   A   L
O   T   N   S
S   I   A   O
R   S   C   N
D W I L L O E H T F O E M A N E H T W I L L B
I   L   A   E
L   O   I   F
L B E S A V E V O R F R E E
        E   D   M
        S

⮞ _ _ _ _ _ _ _ _   _ _ _   _ _ _ _ _

_ _ _   _ _ _ _   _ _   _ _ _   _ _ _ _

_ _ _ _   _ _   _ _ _ _ _ .

9

KEY VERSE

Romans 10:13

A BIG PROMISE

Jesus told His disciples what they should do to receive the gift He was sending to them. Decode the words to complete this wonderful promise Jesus made.

Jesus told His disciples…

It is _____ in _____ that _____ would _____ and would _____ _____ from the dead on the _____ _____. It is also _____ that it would be _____ to ___ _____ that _____ need to _____ and be _____ of their _____. You are _____ that these things _____ _____. Now I will _____ you the _____ _____ to give you _____ if you will _____ in the city of _____.

KEY

A	C	D	E	F	G	H	I	J	L	M
𝄞	▥	†	✕	𝄪	𝄐	∞	⌐	⌀	⊔	✿

N	O	P	R	S	T	U	V	W	Y
Ϸ	𝄂	‖	𝄐	𝄐	𝄐	∞	𝄐	⋏	☯

Luke 24:46–49

A Great Helper

HOLY SPIRIT

Use the picture and letter in each box to figure out the word. Then fit the words in the correct spaces to complete the sentence below.

1. -L

2. -der+rit

3. -B+T

4.

5. -K

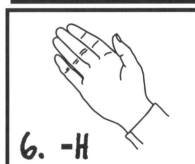

6. -H

7. -SL+GU

8. -T+W

9. -CK+TH

This _____ _____ will _____
　　　　　1.　　　　　　　　　　2.　　　　　　　　　　3.

_____ when you _____ _____
　　4.　　　　　　　　　　　　　　　5.　　　　　　　　　6.

_____ you to _____ _____ .
　　7.　　　　　　　　　　　　　　8.　　　　　　　　9.

11

KEY VERSE

John 16:7,8,13

HOLY SPIRIT

A New Language

Follow the directions. Then write on the lines the words left in the boxes to see a wonderful thing that happened to believers after Jesus went back to heaven.

1. Cross off all words that have an **X** in them.
2. Cross off all words that begin with the letter **C**.
3. Cross off all words that rhyme with dime.
4. Cross off all words that are Bible books.
5. Cross off all words that are animals.
6. Cross off all words that are colors.
7. Cross off all words that are numbers.
8. Cross off all words that end with the letter **P**.

CENT	LIME	MARK	THEY	AX	DOG	WERE	TIME	BOX	ALL
FILLED	BLUE	WITH	THE	TWO	RAP	HOLY	EZRA	SPIRIT	MOUSE
FLAP	AND	RED	FOUR	BEGAN	LAMB	TO	FIVE	WHITE	SPEAK
COMB	RUTH	KINGS	IN	SIP	SIX	OTHER	DIP	LAN-GUAGES	YELLOW

_____ _____ _____ _____ _____

_____ _____ _____ _____ _____

_____ _____ _____ _____ _____

KEY VERSE

Acts 2:4

...And For Kids

In the dove shape color blue all the spaces that have the number 2. Color red all the spaces in the flame shape that have the number 4. Use the words that appear to fill in the spaces below to complete the sentence about what must happen before a person can be baptized in the Holy Spirit.

We must _____ _____ _____ and _____

_____ before we can be baptized in the Holy Spirit.

13

KEY VERSE
ACTS 2:38,39

SECOND COMING

A Great House

Fold the paper so dotted line "**A**" meets dotted line "**B**." Read God's promise for people who trust in Him.

| A → | B |

I AM GOING SEE HOW I AM THERE TO
PREPARE A AFTER FOR YOU PLACE FOR
EACH OF YOU. ON THE PREPARE AFTER I HAVE
DONE THIS, I SEE HIM BACK WILL COME
BACK AND TAK EN BY THE CLOS E YOU WITH
ME. THEN WE OK I WILL DO WILL BE
TOGETHER. Y OUR PLACE WE TH OU KNOW THE
WAY TO WHER ON THE PREPAR E I AM GOING.

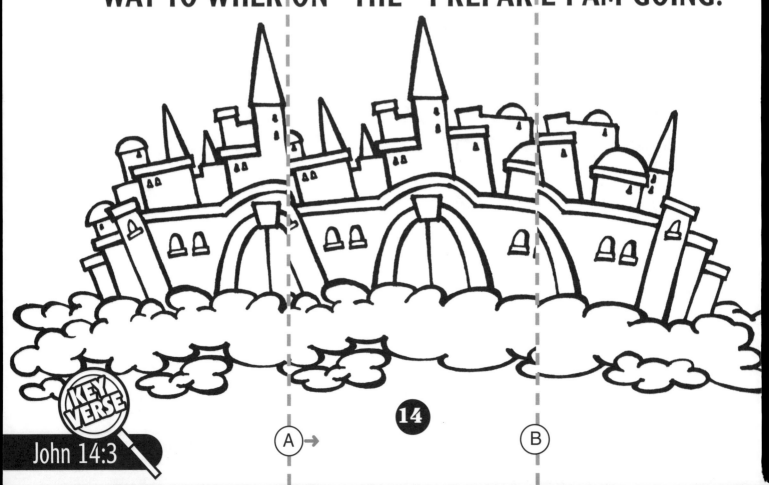

KEY VERSE

John 14:3

A → B

A GREAT DAY!

Use the graph and write the words on the lines. Then read about the awesome event that will happen to all true believers. The letter below each line indicates the row, and the number indicates the column where that word can be found.

	1	2	3	4	5	6
A	CAUGHT	CHURCH	TO	IN	BIBLE	THEM
B	RAPTURE	THAT	AIR	ALIVE	USES	READY
C	CLOUDS	AND	WILL	WHO	THE	
D	BELIEVERS	ALL	OF	MEAN	UP	
E	RETURNS	MEET	BE	ARE	JESUS	
F	TOGETHER	PHRASE	WHEN	IS	WITH	

, "

"

C5	A5	B5	C5	F2	A1	D5	F1
A3	D4	B1	D3	C5	A2	B2	F4
F3	E5	E1	A4	C5	C1	C2	D2
D1	C4	E4	B4	C3	E3	A1	D5
F1	F5	A6	A3	E2	E5	A4	C5
B3	E3	B6					

!

15

KEY VERSE

1 Thessalonians 4:16,17

A Great Life

Begin at start. Follow the circuit line. Each time you come to a letter, write it on the lines below to complete the sentences that tell us something about the future.

Start

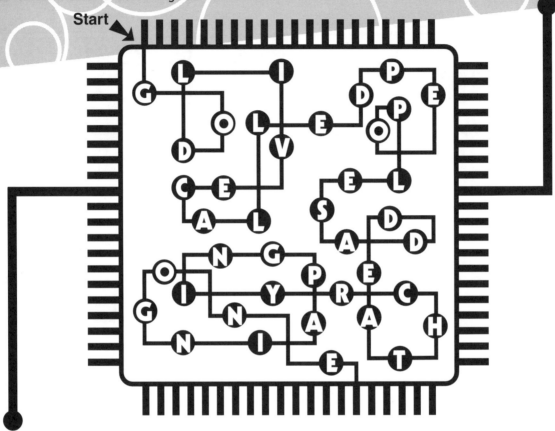

John saw a vision and heard a loud voice from heaven that said: Behold, __ __ __ is coming to __ __ __ __ __ among men. He will live with them and they will be __ __ __ __ __ __ __ __ his __ __ __ __ __ __ __. Because God lives there, no one will be __ __ __. There will not be any __ __ __ __ __. There will not be any __ __ __ __ __ __ __. There will not be any __ __ __ __. All these things will be __ __ __ __ __.

KEY VERSE

16

Revelation 21:3,4